Teaching Reading

A Balanced, Comprehensive Approach to Teaching Reading
in Prekindergarten Through Grade Three

Publishing Information

When *Teaching Reading* was approved by the California State Board of
Education, the members of the State Board were Yvonne W. Larsen,
President; Jerry Hume, Vice-President; Kathryn Dronenburg; Elaine
Lockshin; S. William Malkasian; Marion McDowell; Janet Nicholas;
Sanford C. Sigoloff; and Gerti B. Thomas.

The members of the California Commission on Teacher Credentialing
were Verna B. Dauterive, Chair; Carolyn Ellner, Vice-Chair; Phillip
Barker; Jerilyn R. Harris; Scott Harvey; Juanita Haugen; Elizabeth Heidig;
Carol Katzman; Patricia Kuhn; Torrie L. Norton; Gary Reed; Edmund
Sutro; Darryl Yagi; and Nancy Zarenda. Ex officio members of the
Commision were Edward DeRoche, Henrietta Schwartz, Erwin Seibel,
and Jon Snyder.

This program advisory was published by the California Department of
Education, 721 Capitol Mall, Sacramento, California (mailing address:
P.O. Box 944272, Sacramento, CA 94244-2720). It was distributed under
the provisions of the Library Distribution Act and *Government Code*
Section 11096.

ISBN 0-8011-1276-1

Ordering Information

Copies of this publication are available for $5.75 each, plus shipping and
handling charges. California residents are charged sales tax. Orders may
be sent to the Bureau of Publications, Sales Unit, California Department of
Education, P.O. Box 271, Sacramento, CA 95812-0271; FAX (916) 323-
0823. Telephone orders will be accepted toll-free (1-800-995-4099) for
credit card purchases only.

Notice

The guidance offered in this program advisory is not binding on local
educational agencies or other entities. Except for any statutes, regulations,
or court decisions that may be referenced herein, the advisory is
exemplary, and compliance with it is not mandatory. (See *Education Code*
Section 33308.5.)

Contents

Acknowledgments v

Introduction 1

The Reading Program 3

  Instructional Components 4

    Phonemic Awareness 4

    Letter Names and Shapes 5

    Systematic, Explicit Phonics 6

    Spelling 8

    Vocabulary Development 9

    Comprehension and Higher-Order Thinking 10

    Appropriate Instructional Materials 11

  Grade-Level Expectations and Examples of Classroom Practices 13

    Prekindergarten 14

    Kindergarten 15

    First Grade 16

    Second Grade 17

    Third Grade 17

  Diagnostic Tools 18

  Intervention 19

Instructional Guidance and Support 22

  Importance of Standards 22

  Professional Development 23

  Program Development 24

Conclusion 25

Appendix 26

Bibliography 33

Acknowledgments

The State Superintendent of Public Instruction and the California Department of Education, the California State Board of Education, and the California Commission on Teacher Credentialing have collaborated to develop this program advisory on early reading instruction. We believe that this advisory will provide the policy direction and instructional guidance needed to support the improvement of reading achievement in California.

All parties involved in developing the advisory believe that the uncommon consensus achieved around this document should send a powerful message to all stakeholders involved in education in California that a change of course in the teaching of reading has occurred. While many districts have pioneered a change of course along the lines suggested here, not all have done so systematically. With this document we hope to ensure that all districts change their course to comply with the suggestions contained in this publication.

The State Superintendent, the State Board, and the Commission on Teacher Credentialing are indebted to the following individuals for their significant contributions to this program advisory: Marilyn Adams, Doug Carnine, Linda Diamond, Adria Klein, Sheila Mandel, John Shefelbine, and Jerry Treadway.

The Superintendent, the Board, and the Commission also wish to thank the following individuals for providing valuable suggestions and insights on the draft document: Helen Faul, Allen Felton, Alice Furry, Bill Furry, Diana Garchow, Linda Grandmaison, Susan Hunt, Cindy

Jacobsen, Carmen Jorgenson, Carol Katzman, Sue Kleinhans, Bill Lynch, G. Reid Lyon, Bertha Pendelton, Carol Pugmire, Barbara Smith, and Jean Williams.

The staff contributing to this document include Ruth McKenna, Patricia Newsome, Glen Thomas, Wendy Harris, Dennis Parker, Diane Levin, Nancy Sullivan, Cindy Magness, Deborah Patterson, Judy White, and Jan Agee (California Department of Education); Sam Swofford, David Wright, Linda Bond, and Marilyn Errett (Commission on Teacher Credentialing); and Greg Geeting (State Board of Education).

Contact Information

California Department of Education
Elementary Teaching and Learning Division
721 Capitol Mall, Third Floor
P. O. Box 944272
Sacramento, CA 94244-2720

State Superintendent of Public
  Instruction
(916) 657-4766

Ruth Ann McKenna
Chief Deputy Superintendent
  for Instructional Services
(916) 653-5875

Patricia H. Newsome
Deputy Superintendent
Curriculum and Instructional
  Leadership Branch
(916) 657-3047

Glen Thomas
Assistant Superintendent
  and Director
Elementary Teaching and
  Learning Division
(916) 657- 3351

Wendy Harris, Manager
Elementary Curriculum Office
(916) 657-3105

Diane Levin, Consultant
Elementary Curriculum Office
(916) 657-5236

Dennis Parker, Manager
Elementary Academic Support
  Office
(916) 657-4685

Nancy Sullivan, Consultant
Elementary Academic Support
  Office
(916) 654-1123

California Commission on Teacher Credentialing
1812 Ninth Street
Sacramento, CA 95814-7000

Linda Bond, Consultant
Teacher Preparation
  and Certification
(916) 327-0586

Marilyn Errett, Consultant
Teacher Preparation
  and Certification
(916) 323-7140

Introduction

The purpose of this program advisory is to provide guidance in the development and implementation of a balanced, comprehensive reading program in prekindergarten through grade three. The document is in direct response to the recommendations outlined in the report of the Superintendent's Reading Task Force, *Every Child a Reader* (September, 1995). It is also designed to support two new statutes, known as the "ABC" bills (Assembly Bill 170, Chapter 765, Statutes of 1995, and Assembly Bill 1504, Chapter 764, Statutes of 1995), which require, in part, that the State Board of Education adopt materials in grades one through eight that include "systematic, explicit phonics, spelling, and basic computational skills." The advisory amplifies both the recommendations of the Reading Task Force report as well as the new requirements in law and is offered as a policy statement rather than as a how-to manual.

The audience for this program advisory includes staff developers, reading specialists, principals, district and county leaders in curriculum and instruction, college and university teacher educators, teachers, parents, community members, and publishers.

With this program advisory, the State Superintendent of Public Instruction, the State Board of Education, and the Commission on Teacher Credentialing express their commitment to reading instruction that conforms to the Reading Task Force report, the new statutes, and sound educational policy. The advisory is one of a number of state efforts designed to initiate a turnaround in the reading performance of California's students.

The content of the document serves as the basis for all California Department of Education efforts related to early literacy and supersedes previous Department guidance related to this topic. Furthermore, it is the State Board's desire that the advisory form the basis for all elementary school and school district plans and activities involving reading, such as those related to Title I, school-based coordination, child development, English language learners, and the statewide REACH project.

There is sufficient guidance now available from research about how children best learn to read and about how successful reading programs work to ensure that virtually every child will learn to read well, at least by the end of third grade. This advisory is offered in support of that goal.

The advisory contains two sections. Part I, "The Reading Program," focuses on the essential components of a complete program of early reading instruction, with specific guidance in systematic, explicit skills instruction and other essential components of an early reading program; classroom diagnosis; program assessment; and early intervention strategies, including family-school partnerships that support student learning and home learning. Grade-level expectations and examples of classroom activities are also included in this part of the advisory.

Part II, "Instructional Guidance and Support," addresses the planning necessary to support classroom implementation, including the development of local standards and ongoing professional development.

The Reading Program

Essential Components of a Balanced and Comprehensive Reading Program—From Research to Practice

The Reading Task Force report called for a balanced and comprehensive approach to early reading instruction that includes both teacher-directed skills instruction and the activities and strategies most often associated with literature-based, integrated language arts instruction. Specifically, on page 2 of its introduction to *Every Child a Reader*, the Reading Task Force states: "It was determined that a balanced and comprehensive approach to reading must have:

(1) a strong literature, language, and comprehension program that includes a balance of oral and written language;

(2) an organized, explicit skills program that includes phonemic awareness (sounds in words), phonics, and decoding skills to address the needs of the emergent reader;

(3) ongoing diagnosis that informs teaching and assessment that ensures accountability; and

(4) a powerful early intervention program that provides individual tutoring for children at risk of reading failure."

This program advisory suggests that explicit skills instruction be part of a broader language-rich program consistent with the best practices of literature-based language arts instruction and the *English–Language Arts Framework*, which is currently under revision. Any changes made to improve or enhance reading instruction and practice should be informed by current research while conforming to relevant statutes.

Instructional Components

To be complete and balanced and to meet the literacy needs of all students, including English language learners and students with special needs, any early reading program must include the following instructional components: phonemic awareness; letter names and shapes; systematic, explicit phonics; spelling; vocabulary development; comprehension and higher-order thinking; and appropriate instructional materials.

Phonemic Awareness

Phonemic awareness is the understanding that spoken words and syllables are themselves made up of sequences of elementary speech sounds. This understanding is essential for learning to read an alphabetic language because it is these elementary sounds or phonemes that letters represent. Without phonemic awareness, phonics can make no sense, and the spellings of words can be learned only by rote.

In the early stages of its development, phonemic awareness does not involve written letters or words and is, therefore, not synonymous with phonics. In later stages, however, work on phonemic awareness and phonics appears to be mutually reinforcing.

Research has shown repeatedly that phonemic awareness is a powerful predictor of success in learning to read. Research findings include the following:

- Phonemic awareness is more highly related to learning to read than are tests of general intelligence, reading readiness, and listening comprehension (Stanovich, 1986, 1993).
- The lack of phonemic awareness is the most powerful determinant of the likelihood of failure to learn to read because of its importance in learning the English alphabetic system or in learning how print represents spoken words. If children cannot hear and manipulate the sounds in spoken words, they have an extremely difficult time learning how to map those sounds to letters and letter patterns—the essence of decoding (Adams, 1990).
- Phonemic awareness is the most important core and causal factor separating normal and disabled readers (Share and Stanovich, 1995).

- Phonemic awareness is equally important in learning to spell. (Ehri, 1992; Treiman, 1993).

As children become proficient in spoken language, they learn to attend to its meaning rather than its sounds. For that reason, acquiring phonemic awareness is difficult for many. However, research demonstrates that phonemic awareness can be fostered through language activities that encourage active exploration and manipulation of sounds and that doing so significantly accelerates both reading and writing growth for all children. Research also indicates that all young readers benefit from explicit assistance with phonemic awareness; at least one-fifth of them depend critically on it. Children should be diagnosed in mid-kindergarten to determine if they are adequately progressing and, if not, given more intensive phonemic awareness training. The discovery of the nature and enabling importance of phonemic awareness is said to be the single greatest breakthrough in reading pedagogy in this century (Adams, 1990).

Support for phonemic awareness development should occur in prekindergarten, kindergarten, and first grade (Yopp, 1992), including the abilities to:

- attend to the separate words of sentences (e.g., rhyming songs, print tracking);
- break up words into syllables (e.g., clapping syllables);
- detect and generate rhymes;
- engage in alliterative language play (e.g., listening for or generating words that begin with a specific initial phoneme);
- blend phonemes to make words (e.g., /b/-/a/-/t/= bat);
- make new words by substituting one phoneme for another (e.g., change the /h/ in "hot" to /p/);
- identify the middle and final phonemes of words; and
- segment words into phonemes (e.g., dog = /d/-/o/-/g/).

Letter Names and Shapes

Familiarity with the letters of the alphabet is another powerful predictor of early reading success. Until children can quickly recognize letters, they cannot begin to appreciate that all words are made of sequences and patterns of letters. Until children can comfortably discriminate the shape of one letter from another, there is no point in teaching letter-sound pairings. Encouraging young children to produce temporary spellings is a powerful means of developing phonemic awareness; yet children will not write willingly until they can form the letters with adequate ease and to their own satisfaction. Knowledge of the letter names is important, too, for it is shown to be a major means by which children recall or generate the sounds of letters in their independent reading and writing.

Because the names and shapes of the letters in English are very similar to one another, their learning is best fostered through numerous guided and playful exposures to the alphabet. Across the prekindergarten and kindergarten years, teachers should create many opportunities to engage their students with the names, shapes, and formation of the letters of the alphabet.

Systematic, Explicit Phonics

This term refers to an organized program where letter-sound correspondences for letters and letter clusters are directly taught; blended; practiced in words, word lists, and word families; and practiced initially in text with a high percentage of decodable words linked to the phonics lesson. Teachers should provide prompt and explicit feedback.

In reading for meaning, skillful readers move their eyes through text left to right, line by line, and word by word. With the exception of short function words, such as *a*, *on*, *of*, and *any*, they almost never skip or guess. Instead, they fixate on very nearly each and every word of text. Further, during the fraction of a second that they do so, they take in—and must take in—all of its letters, translating them to speech sounds on their way to evoking the word's meaning.

These word recognition processes are far too rapid and automatic for skillful readers to be aware of them. Nevertheless, their reality has been broadly confirmed through a variety of technologically sophisticated research methods with mature readers, including eye-movement recordings and brain-imaging techniques.

In terms of instruction, these findings carry a critical implication. To become skillful readers, children must learn how to decode words instantly and effortlessly. It is for this reason that children must be taught initially to examine the letters and letter patterns of every new word while reading. Similarly, while practicing phonetic decoding, children must not be taught to skip new words or guess their meaning. While the interpretation of text depends integrally on context, the recognition of its words should not. Research reveals that only poor and disabled readers rely on context for word identification (Stanovich, 1980). Conversely, poorly developed knowledge of spellings and spelling-sound correspondences is found to be the most frequent, debilitating, and pervasive cause of reading difficulty (Bruck, 1990; Perfetti, 1985; Rack, Snowling, & Olson, 1992; Vellutino, 1991). Young readers must develop fast, accurate decoding skills; and research verifies that they are much more likely to do so if they receive a good program of phonics instruction.

The role of effective phonics instruction is to help children understand, apply, and learn the alphabetic principle and conventions of written language. Phonics instruction is not about rote drill involving a comprehensive list of spelling-sound correspondences and phonics rules. The most effective phonics instruction is explicit—that is, taking care to clarify key points and principles for students. In addition, it is systematic—that is, it gradually builds from basic elements to more subtle and complex patterns. The goal is to convey the logic of the system and to invite its extension to new words that the children will encounter on their own. Teaching phonics opportunistically by pointing out spelling-sound connections only as they arise does not have the same impact on learning.

Research shows that children are naturally inclined to view words as holistic patterns, rather like pictures. The drawback to this approach is that learning to recognize one word as a picture offers no advantage toward learning to recognize the next. Toward developing children's word recognition abilities, it follows that among the first and most critical challenges is that of persuading children to go beyond this tendency.

By its very nature, phonics instruction encourages children to examine all the letters of each new word, left to right. Conversely, by linking speech sounds to the letters, it enables students to use their oral knowledge of a word to remember the word's spelling. In addition, it provides a strategy by which students can identify previously unseen words on their own as they read.

Initial phonics instruction is best conducted with a relatively small set of consonants and short vowels. These spelling-sound relationships should be developed progressively. By using this limited set of letters to build as many familiar words as possible, students can be convinced of the utility of phonics and shown that every letter matters. Most commonly, initial lessons should focus on short words that adhere to the basic left-to-right principle of sounding and blending, such as *fat* and *fit*. Once children have learned to sound out such basic short-vowel patterns, lessons should be extended to include the most common other vowel spellings. Importantly, research demonstrates that for children who understand how the alphabetic principle works, it is relatively easy for them to add new letter-sound pairs to the working set.

Research shows that it is important for children to practice the phonics they have learned. It is therefore essential that the initial books that children attempt to read on their own be composed of decodable text. More details on this subject are provided in the section entitled "Appropriate Instructional Materials."

Not all words are amenable to decoding. Whether irregular or not, those short words of extremely high frequency, such as *the*, *of*, *are*, and *you*, should be familiarized at the outset. Text cannot be written without these very high frequency words. Further, because so many of them are irregularly spelled, they should be recognized at a glance so that the student's attention is not diverted from decoding. A workable number of these words should be firmly established in kindergarten and early first grade by directing attention to them in big book and writing activities. As other irregular words are added along the way, it is worth noting their peculiarities as well as their phonetic regularities. This practice serves at once to make them more memorable and to protect the rest of the system from their waywardness.

Context has been shown to have a powerful effect on students' comprehension of words and sentences. The use of syntactic (grammar) and semantic (meaning) levels of language has been found to be helpful in a number of ways. Sometimes a reader will use context cues when learning decoding skills. Context is also useful to resolve ambiguity (e.g., in the two pronunciations of the word *read*). A third use is to suggest a possible meaning when a word is unknown to the reader (e.g., the meaning of *facade* when the reader does not know that *facade* means the front or face of a building). Finally, context helps accelerate reading rate. Large quantities of a variety of genres (e.g., novel, biography, short story, play, poem, article) of fiction and nonfiction materials must be read each year by each child beginning in grade one. Fluency with text is the ultimate key to the door of comprehension and higher-order thinking.

The best instruction provides a strong relationship between what children learn in phonics and what they read. A high proportion of the words in the earliest selections children read should be decodable (i.e., conform to the phonics they have already been taught; *Becoming a Nation of Readers,* 1984). After children have demonstrated initial levels of phonemic awareness, both phonemic awareness and phonics can be taught simultaneously. At this point it is also essential that both phonemic awareness and phonics be mutually reinforced in the context of integrated, shared reading and writing activities.

Spelling

Good spelling is much more than a literary nicety. Poorly developed spelling knowledge is shown to hinder children's writing, to disrupt their reading fluency, and to obstruct their vocabulary development (Adams, Treiman, & Pressley, 1996; Read, 1986). Although it is appropriate to encourage beginners to use temporary or invented spellings to express their thoughts in print, programmatic instruction in correct spellings should begin in first grade and continue across the school years. In addition, and increasingly across the school years, children should be expected to attend to the correctness of their spellings in their writing.

Children's temporary spellings are a direct reflection of their own knowledge and understanding of how words actually are spelled. As such, they are also an invaluable medium for diagnosing difficulties and evaluating progress. For example, children who scribble need support with print awareness and letter knowledge.

By engaging students in thinking actively and reflectively about the sounds of words and their spellings, exercise in temporary spelling lays a strong cognitive foundation for both formal spelling and phonics. It does not, however, eliminate the need for learning how to spell correctly. Consistent with this, research demonstrates that combining ample early support of temporary spelling with systematic, formal spelling instruction results in more rapid growth in both correct spelling and word recognition than does either approach alone (Shefelbine, 1995).

Regular and active attention to spelling in the classroom serves to increase the willingness and productivity with which all students write.

Because the first challenge is to develop the children's phonemic awareness and knowledge of basic letter-sound correspondences, such activities should begin with short, regular words, such as *pot*, *pat*, and *pan*. As the principal goal of these early sessions is to develop the kind of thinking on which good spelling depends, they should be playful and exploratory. Beyond challenging the children to produce the spellings in focus, the lessons should be designed to model the process of generating and troubleshooting one's spellings and to provide instructive feedback on specific difficulties.

Gradually, the focus of these instructional activities should be extended to more complex spelling patterns and words. Moving pattern by pattern from basics through consonant blends, long vowel spellings, inflections, and so on, the primary goal is to instill the larger logic and regularities of the system and its conventions. The early exploratory lessons will evolve seamlessly into formal spelling instruction.

In later grades, such instruction should extend to spellings and meanings of prefixes, suffixes, and word roots. Leading children to notice such patterns across many different examples makes it easier for them to learn the particular words in study. At the same time, it supports their ability to look for and use such spelling patterns and word analysis strategies beyond the lesson in their own reading and writing.

The primary goal of spelling instruction, as with phonics, is to alert children to patterns, to how words are put together, and to conventions and correctness. Spelling lists and quizzes should be purposeful and support and reinforce reading and writing instruction. Extensive reading and writing, including opportunities to edit for final publication, for real purposes and audiences, play an indispensable role in mastering spelling.

Vocabulary Development

Written language places far greater demands on people's vocabulary knowledge than does casual spoken language. Indeed, more advanced texts depend so heavily on precise wording to build meaning and message that, from the middle grades on, students' reading comprehension can be closely estimated by measures of their vocabulary. Students will be able to learn from these texts only if they approach them with most of the vocabulary they require.

In fact, learning to read brings with it special opportunities as well as special needs for expanding one's vocabulary. Thus, research indicates that of the roughly 3,000 new words that the average student learns per year, the majority are learned by encountering them in text. However, the number of new words that children can learn from text depends on how much they read, and the amount that children read ranges enormously. As documented by research, the ninetieth percentile fifth grader reads about 200 times more text per year than the tenth percentile reader does (Nagy, Herman, & Anderson, 1985).

In the interest of vocabulary development, then, all children should be read to as much as possible. Yet this cannot be the whole solution.

First, children need to be encouraged to attend to the meanings of new words they encounter in text. Second, the ability to understand and remember the meanings of new words depends quite strongly on how well developed one's vocabulary is already.

Beginning in kindergarten, vocabulary growth should be actively supported in the classroom. Vocabulary instruction is shown to be most effective when explicit information about the words' definitions is complemented by attention to their usages and shades of meaning across contexts. It is useful to organize vocabulary studies structurally, in terms of roots and affixes, or topically (e.g., science, transportation, weather, or math words). In addition, children should be asked to create glossaries of the new words they encounter in their reading. Bear in mind that the ultimate goal of such instruction is no more to teach new words than to teach children to learn them on their own.

Comprehension and Higher-Order Thinking

When we read effortlessly and accurately, we are able to construct meaning at two levels. The first level works with the words of the text and gives us back a literal understanding of what the author has written. Yet productive reading involves far more than literal comprehension. The priority issues while reading should include the following questions: Why am I reading this and how does this information relate to my reasons for so doing? What is the author's point of view? What are the underlying assumptions? Do I understand what the author is saying and why? Do I know where the author is headed? Is the text internally consistent? Is it consistent with what I already know and believe or have learned elsewhere? If not, where does it depart and what do I think about the discrepancy? It is the second level of meaning construction that yields this sort of reflective, purposeful understanding.

The productivity of students' higher-order comprehension processes is limited by their vocabulary and reading fluency in two ways. First, these higher-order processes are necessarily thought-intensive. They require analytic, evaluative, and reflective access to local and long-term memory.

Yet active attention is limited. To the extent that readers struggle with the words, they necessarily lose track of meaning. Second, it is the wording or explicitly given information in the text that constitutes the basic data with which the higher-order comprehension processes must work. When readers skip or fail to understand the words of the text, comprehension suffers.

In the interest of developing students' reading comprehension, the students should be given many opportunities for open discussion of both the highlights and difficulties of text. Because the grammatical structures of written text are more varied and complex than those of casual, oral language, regular exploration and explicit instruction on formal syntax are also warranted. Research shows, too, that children's reflective control of text can be improved through direct instruction in comprehension strategies. These sorts of discussions and activities should be conducted throughout a range of literary genres, both fiction and nonfiction. Beginning in kindergarten, they should be a regular part of the language arts curriculum throughout the children's school years.

Even so, the single most valuable activity for developing children's comprehension is reading itself. The amount of reading that children do is shown to predict the growth in reading comprehension across the elementary school years even after controlling for entry-level differences. It predicts the quantity as well as the language, vocabulary, and structure of students' writing. It also predicts the richness of their oral storytelling. Among older students and adults, it predicts receptive vocabulary, verbal fluency, content-area achievement, and all manner of general knowledge even when other measures of school ability, general intelligence, age, education, and reading comprehension itself are taken out of the equation (Anderson et al., 1984; Adams, Treiman, & Pressley, 1996; Stanovich, 1993). Through reading, students encounter new words, new language, and new facts. Beyond that, however, they encounter thoughts and modes of thinking that might never arise in their face-to-face worlds. In the interest of their own greatest potential and fulfillment, all students should be encouraged to read as frequently, broadly, and thoughtfully as possible.

Appropriate Instructional Materials

A balanced, comprehensive early literacy program must embrace a variety of reading materials. To illustrate the range, these may include environmental print, student compositions, classroom anthologies, trade books (e.g., literature books that are not part of a traditional textbook series), chapter books, core works of fiction and nonfiction, magazines, newspapers, reference materials, and technology. Whatever the nature of the material, however, the mode in which it is read can be roughly divided into three categories: read-alouds, instructional reading, and independent reading. Beyond its content, the instructional value of any given text depends jointly on the developmental level of the students and the mode in which the text is to be read.

Reading aloud to students is important at every age. Its principal purpose is not to replace the time spent reading independently but rather to open their literary worlds by helping them to learn about what they are yet to learn. In view of this purpose, materials that are most appropriate for read-alouds are materials that, while capturing the students' interests, are also still beyond their ability to read and digest on their own. Thus, whereas illustrated storybooks are most suitable for kindergartners, longer stories and even well-chosen novels are within reach by the end of first grade. Choose stories, chapter books, and poems; but also choose reference books and news clippings; math, science, and history; biographies; jokes and brainteasers. Use read-aloud sessions as a means of helping students to explore genre, language, and information. The goal is to whet their appetites, open their curiosity, kindle their knowledge, and show them the horizons.

For preschoolers and kindergartners, the most appropriate materials for teaching concepts about print and sight words are big books, especially those with predictable or familiar texts (Clay, 1993; Holdaway, 1979). Encouraging children to match the wording to the text in these materials is invaluable in fostering their print awareness and syntactic growth. Big books with repeated word patterns are also good resources for helping children learn to recognize very high frequency words.

Across the later grades, materials selected for instructional reading sessions are to be read by students but with help by adults. The purpose of these sessions is to be proactive; they are forums for stretching the students, for showing them—with adult guidance and feedback—how to handle new textual challenges. In general, the most appropriate materials for instructional sessions should be just a bit more difficult than what the students can read competently on their own. Bear in mind that texts can be difficult in many different ways—in wording, language, concept or information, genre, story structure, or message. As a rule of thumb, if a text is hard in one way, it should best be manageable in all others. In that way, the students have the best chance of appreciating and coming to terms with the lesson, rather than losing interest or getting lost.

When English language learners begin to learn to read in English, either as their first reading experience or after learning to read in their home language, they can be most successful learning to read what they can already say and understand. As with all other learners, decodable texts should be used to provide these early readers practice in becoming fluent and accurate decoders. Reading decodable and patterned texts, however, must be preceded by sufficient oral language development relative to those texts to ensure success in reading with such materials.

The goal of all reading sessions is to support students' interest and capacity for independent reading. Research strongly asserts that from the beginning of first grade and in tandem with basic phonics instruction, the most appropriate materials for independent reading are decodable texts. Toward creating a solid foundation for learning to read, most new words in these texts should be wholly decodable on the basis of the phonics that students have been taught. Sight words should be familiarized ahead of time so that they will not divert this purpose. As soon as children can read such basic decodable texts with reasonable comfort and fluency, they can move on to less controlled texts such as trade books. Some students will be ready to do so sooner than others. However, by having an ample supply of decodable texts and easy-to-read materials, it is possible to ensure that all students are productively engaged.

To encourage optimal progress with the use of any of these early reading materials, teachers need to be aware of the difficulty level of the text relative to a child's reading level. A book is said to be at a child's independent level if 95–100 percent of the words can be read correctly.

Instructional level books can be read with a 90–94 percent level of accuracy. Frustration level reading involves text read by a child at the 89 percent accuracy level or below. Regardless of how well a child already reads, high error rates are negatively correlated with growth; low error rates are positively linked with growth. A text that is too difficult, then, not only serves to undermine a child's confidence and will but also diminishes learning itself.

An effective program depends equally on establishing time and expectation for independent reading. In the beginning, partner or small-group reading may work better than asking children to use their time well on their own. When sending materials home with beginners, teachers should encourage the parents to share-read (e.g., every other sentence or paragraph) with their children. Remember, too, that for all materials to be read by children, rereading is of enormous benefit. Returning to a text after several days or even weeks is a very good tactic for young readers (Clay, 1991). Research shows that rereadings result in marked improvements not just in children's speed, accuracy, and expression but also in their comprehension and linguistic growth. Rereadings bring not only the opportunity for fluency and the learning thus fostered but also a chance to revisit and reflect on the meaning, message, and language of a text. Finally, because classroom time is limited and because literacy growth depends so strongly on the amount of reading children do, **all students in every grade should be required to read every day outside of school.**

Grade-Level Expectations and Examples of Classroom Practices

As districts consider making changes to address the essential components of a powerful reading program, careful planning needs to occur to ensure appropriate progression across the grade spans. Examples of grade-level expectations and learning activities to support student learning in these areas are included below; these examples are intended to be illustrative, providing districts insights into concepts that should be addressed at each grade level. More detailed information regarding grade-level expectations is provided in the appendix to the Reading Task Force report entitled "Sample Reading Curriculum Timeline: Preschool Through Eighth Grade," which is reprinted on pages 26–32 of this publication.

In order to meet the individual needs of all learners, each classroom should provide a balance of grouping types. Children are organized in whole groups, small groups, pairs, or as individuals for guided process reading and writing, shared reading, skills instruction, and independent reading and writing. In addition to planning their programs carefully, districts need to ensure that all teachers understand the importance of flexible grouping in the teaching of reading. It is usually not efficient or effective for teachers to teach reading across the span of skill levels represented in an entire class of students. Flexible grouping helps teachers match instruction to the widely differing skill levels typically found in a classroom. Flexible groups are skill based and temporary, allowing instruction to align as much as possible with the skill level of those children in the group; children who learn at a faster or slower rate move to a different group as needed.

Prekindergarten

Grade-level expectations. Before entering kindergarten, virtually every child should:

- recognize print in the environment;
- distinguish separate words;
- recognize rhyming words;
- know some letter names and shapes, including the letters in the child's name;
- begin to demonstrate reading-like behaviors, such as pretending to read and write;
- begin to demonstrate understanding of picture books and simple stories; and
- retell stories, make predictions, and connect stories to background experiences in a teacher-guided group format.

Learning Activities. At the prekindergarten level, language arts skills and understandings are developed primarily through a variety of interactive activities, such as painting, drawing, building with blocks, singing, dancing, and dramatic play. Children are read picture books and simple storybooks every day at school, and parents are encouraged to read to their children at home. Activities provide playful yet explicit exposure to letter names and the alphabet. Examples of learning activities for this age group include:

- singing nursery rhymes and songs, including playful songs which substitute sounds in words and play with word parts;
- using language in play, such as playing house or pretending to write a grocery list;
- playing rhyming games (singing songs and reciting poems or other text);
- playing with magnetic letters or letter blocks; and
- having guided discussion of read-alouds and other shared experiences.

Kindergarten

Grade-level expectations. At the end of kindergarten, virtually every child should:

- have mastered all of the concepts about print, including the names and shapes of most of the letters of the alphabet;
- demonstrate phonemic awareness through activities such as rhyming, clapping syllables, substituting sounds, and blending phonemes;
- recognize upper and lower case letters;
- know how to read his/her own and others' names and common environmental print in the classroom;
- read some high-frequency words;
- read the first few levels of decodable readers for kindergarten;
- write independently at the alphabetic stage of development;
- retell in simple terms stories that have been read to him/her as well as make simple evaluations and interpretations of their content; and
- connect, with the teacher's help, what is read to him/her with real experiences.

Learning activities. At the kindergarten level, language arts skills and understandings are still developed primarily through a variety of interactive language activities. Students are immersed in a print-rich environment. Activities capitalize on children's natural curiosity and sense of playfulness; they provide extensive exposure to the alphabet and promote phonemic awareness. Children are read to every day, both at school and at home, and are exposed to a wide range of materials, including picture books, storybooks, poems, and expository text. Students also have daily writing opportunities. Examples of learning activities for this age group include:

- playing games that identify words that do not belong and singing songs and reciting texts that play with phonemes or that substitute words and word parts in a rhyming pattern;
- using physical responses, such as clapping, tapping, and body movements, to demonstrate syllabication or patterns in songs, stories, or words;
- sorting letters or identifying prominent letters in words;
- having guided discussion of read-alouds and other shared experiences;
- singing and reciting verses;
- staging class performances of stories and nursery rhymes;
- "reading" predictable books independently;
- tracing letters in sand; making letters out of clay; playing with letter blocks, magnetic letters, and pocket charts;
- writing in journals and dictating stories;
- discussing word meanings, ideas, books, and experiences; and
- using a language experience approach to reading activities.

First Grade

Grade-level expectations. At the end of first grade, virtually every child should:

- demonstrate phonemic awareness and knowledge of how print is organized;
- demonstrate fluent and accurate decoding skills with grade-level materials;
- read independently grade-level materials that contain the most common sight words and employ knowledge of most consonants, short vowels, and the silent "e" rule;
- use conventional spelling for simple, regularly spelled words as well as temporary spelling for more complex words;
- identify all letter names and shapes;
- retell stories he/she has read with a beginning, middle, and end;
- relate parts of stories to his/her own experience and tell about the parts liked best and why; and
- make predictions about what is read to him/her or what he/she has read.

Learning activities. At the first-grade level, students continue to be immersed in a print-rich environment. Children are read to and practice their own reading on a daily basis. Students have daily writing opportunities. Activities include play with language and are structured so as to promote phonemic awareness, letter recognition, and comprehension. Direct, explicit phonics instruction is provided, and formal spelling instruction should be introduced late in the year. Examples of learning activities for this age group include:

- separating words into separate sounds;
- providing multiple opportunities first to read decodable text and eventually to read predictable text and easy trade books;
- participating in daily word play in which small groups of students construct words by changing the beginning, middle, or ending of more complex words;
- blending letters when learning common spelling and sound patterns;
- decoding big words by decoding smaller words or word parts within them;
- writing in stories or recording observations, using conventional spelling for simple, regularly spelled words as well as temporary spelling for more complex words;
- maintaining a reading log of leveled books read independently, showing reading of increasingly complex text;
- writing captions for pictures;
- making storyboards or other graphic organizers with others that show the setting, characters, and events in a story;
- engaging in shared, guided, and independent reading and writing;
- using a language experience approach to reading activities; and

- having guided discussions focused on comprehension and thinking.

Second Grade

Grade-level expectations. At the end of second grade, virtually every child should:

- read grade-level materials independently;
- demonstrate mastery of most phonics elements (e.g., consonants, vowels, blends, clusters, syllables, common phonics rules);
- use conventional spelling in his/her own writing for high-frequency words and words with regular spelling patterns;
- connect readings to experiences or knowledge; and
- ask test-like questions about what has been read, clarify new terms in context, confirm predictions, summarize, interpret, and analyze the content in simple terms.

Learning activities. At the second grade level, students continue to be immersed in a print-rich environment. Direct, explicit phonics instruction and formal spelling instruction are provided. Children are read to and read independently every day. Students have daily writing opportunities, and activities are structured to promote reading comprehension. Examples of learning activities for this age group include:

- changing or deleting the beginning, middle, and ending sounds of words in a pocket chart to make new words;
- decoding more complex words in a shared reading;
- writing an imaginative story or a letter, using conventional spelling;
- maintaining a reading log of books read independently, showing reading of increasingly complex texts;
- engaging in word studies and maintaining word logs for spelling and vocabulary development;
- participating in shared, guided, and independent reading and writing;
- participating in a choral reading performance for parents or other students; and
- participating in discussions and writing that develop comprehension and thinking skills.

Third Grade

Grade-level expectations. At the end of third grade, virtually every child should:

- read independently grade-level fiction and nonfiction materials with literal and inferential comprehension;
- develop a knowledge of common spelling patterns, roots, and affixes;

- use conventional spelling and conventions of print (paragraphs, end-sentence punctuation);
- question; clarify new words; make predictions and answer "if-then" questions; summarize reading passages; and answer questions that require analysis, synthesis, and evaluation of grade-level fiction and nonfiction material; and
- support answers to questions about the reading by drawing on background knowledge and upon literal and inferential information from the text.

Learning activities. At the third grade level, students should continue to be immersed in a print-rich environment. Children are read to and read independently every day in school and at home. Students have daily writing opportunities. Direct, explicit phonics instruction and formal spelling instruction are provided. Activities are also structured to promote reading comprehension. Examples of learning activities for this age group include:

- reading aloud to a partner with rhythm, pace, and intonation that sounds like natural speech;
- maintaining a reading log of books read independently, showing reading of increasingly complex texts;
- writing a report based upon reading about a topic in several sources that includes appropriate facts and uses conventional spelling and conventions of print (paragraphs, end-sentence punctuation);
- engaging in word studies and maintaining word logs for spelling and vocabulary development;
- doing process writing for different purposes and audiences that develops higher-order thinking; and
- participating in guided and independent discussions that promote effective comprehension strategies and higher-order thinking.

Diagnostic Tools

In Recommendation 2 of its report, the Reading Task Force stated that schools and school districts should provide every teacher with a variety of assessment tools and strategies necessary to inform daily instruction. Student skills can be assessed with a list that begins with single letters and progresses to words ordered in complexity. Text used for the assessment of fluency and comprehension should be ordered with respect to difficulty as well. By assessing these measures three or four times a year with children in kindergarten through grade 2, teachers can detect which children are falling behind in classroom instruction and are candidates for early intervention. Other useful tools include:

- screening assessments (e.g., for phonemic awareness, language proficiency in English or other home languages, concepts about print, and writing);
- checklists (especially in kindergarten for areas such as concepts about print, phonemic awareness, letter knowledge and phonics, and attitudes toward reading and writing);
- "running records" for assessing reading accuracy, analyzing student errors, and establishing reading level;
- scoring guides for writing (including benchmarks indicating "competence");
- records of amount of reading or writing accomplished in terms of pages, minutes, words, stories, books, and so forth;
- individual and group-administered tests, including unit tests that accompany adopted reading programs, quick assessments, reading inventories, and annual norm-referenced assessments;
- comprehensive assessments, such as the *California Learning Record*; and
- collections of student work (rated on rubrics that include benchmarks indicating "competence").

Such assessments might be conducted more frequently for children who are struggling and are considered below grade level and less frequently for those achieving at higher levels. In addition, the results of such assessments can be used in at least two ways. One obvious use is to guide instruction by determining what a given child has not yet learned. Over time, information viewed in this way will form the basis for a teacher's decision to seek interventions beyond the classroom to accelerate a child's development to a level comparable to his/her peers. A second and equally important use of diagnostic information is to determine what a child already knows so that it might be explicitly reinforced whenever possible. Using information in this way guides the teacher to strengthen the skill or concept and to build a student's confidence and awareness of what he/she knows and can do. In short, "diagnosis" as used in this document refers to ways to collect and use information on students' strengths and their weaknesses for the purposes of both **classroom instruction** as well as **decisions for providing early interventions.**

Intervention

Although the program features outlined above might be research based, balanced, and comprehensive, it is a significant challenge for a single teacher to ensure the success of every child in reading through the classroom experiences. Children arrive at school with literacy experiences that range from zero to 2000 hours. Some also speak multiple languages and all bring a variety of different background experiences with them. Given these realities, it is going to take the school, community, and parents working together to achieve success in reading and thinking for every child in California.

The Reading Task Force recognized this need in Recommendation 3:

> Schools must have an effective, rigorous, proven intervention program as part of their comprehensive literacy plan for instruction, with an emphasis on early intervention for children by mid-first grade.

The first level of intervention is the classroom with a powerful program of rich language and instruction. Diagnostic information collected daily, weekly, and monthly by the teacher will indicate which children are beginning to struggle and lag behind their peers. Except for phonemic awareness screening and intervention in kindergarten, early intervention in reading will usually begin in the first grade. Differential treatment of children by the teacher should be a first response. Providing extra help for the lowest-performing students can be done in several ways. Examples of in-class interventions include organizing one-on-one and small-group work by the teacher, collecting diagnostic information more frequently, providing guided reading instruction five times a week for some children and two or three times for others working on level, and enlisting extra tutorial help from instructional aides and cross-age tutors, parents, or community members.

A second level of intervention occurs outside of class. Participation in such intervention often is preceded by more formal diagnostic measures and assessments conducted by specialists or by a Student Study Team process. Such help always involves parents as partners to the degree they can participate. Home activities should include extra reading, writing, and high-quality conversations with parents and older siblings. Categorical programs and the funds associated with them also represent a source of support for in-class supplemental help, pullout, before-and after-school, intersession, and summer programs. Summer programs and intersessions provide a particularly strong opportunity for more intensive instruction for the lowest-achieving students to allow them to proceed with their group or class into the next level.

The most effective interventions typically have the following characteristics:

- They are applied as early as possible in a child's educational career, but not before there has been an opportunity for effective classroom instruction to be tried first.
- They involve well-trained specialists.
- They are more intense than the typical classroom experience, providing personalized, assessment-based instruction; more time

and practice on selected skills, concepts, and strategies; and smaller adult-student ratios.

- They are effective as gap-closing strategies for low achievers.
- They are short lived, consistently applied, and finite in duration. For example, one strategy might be designed to last for 20 days, another for 15 weeks, and yet another for 60 sessions.

Finally, it is important to review special education placement within the school. As the Reading Task Force report indicated, "Too many students placed in special education have reading problems that could have been prevented. Before students with reading problems are referred for special education, a series of in-class or out-of-class short-term interventions, such as tutoring, should be utilized. Special education resources can then focus on those students who truly have long-term, ongoing special needs" (p. 6). It is critical that special education students receive the same powerful instruction as other students receive. In addition, special education students must be given more time and opportunities to practice.

To meet the intent of the Reading Task Force, school communities will need to focus on the performance of individual children as opposed to just raising grade-level school averages. The most successful communities have been relentless in their commitment to every student meeting high, clearly articulated reading expectations at each grade level, and certainly no later than by the end of grade three. In fact, there is good evidence to suggest that a child's entire educational career depends on just this kind of approach.

Instructional Guidance and Support

Importance of Standards

Increasingly, state and national reports call for improved results for students by setting high standards and adopting clear accountability measures. The Reading Task Force endorsed the Education Commission of the States' report, *Rising to the Challenge* (1995), which recommended that California establish statewide standards for kindergarten through twelfth grade, build a new statewide assessment system around those standards, and develop an accountability process that emphasizes local responsibility for improving student achievement.

Assembly Bill 265 (Chapter 975, Statutes of 1995) calls for such standards and statewide assessment. Until those standards are available, however, and until they are adopted by the State Board of Education (by January 1, 1998, as required in AB 265), districts are encouraged to adopt their own grade-level content and performance standards in reading, writing, speaking, and listening, with the goal of having every student reading independently and comprehending fully no later than the end of third grade. As a resource for establishing local standards, districts may want to use the *"Draft Interim Content and Performance Standards,"* generated by the network of Challenge districts. Standards for mathematics and English–language arts are currently being revised by the network and are due to be released in late summer, 1996; but copies of the version released in January, 1996, can be obtained from the Bureau of Publications, Sales Unit, California Department of Education. The standards are also available on the California Department of Education's World Wide Web site:

http://goldmine.cde.ca.gov/WWW/Challenge_Standards/
Challenge_Standards.html

A new version of these standards will be posted on the web site when they are released.

Similarly, in the absence of a statewide system of assessment and accountability, local school boards are encouraged to adopt a local system for tracking performance. More importantly, in recognition of the critical role of the teacher, local boards and districts need to have in place mechanisms for ongoing teacher support and training. This support and training must be designed explicitly to address attainment of grade-level standards by students as measured by the local accountability system.

Professional Development

In-service training within school districts in California is often scheduled around the instructional materials adoption in a subject area each year. Any district following this model would offer in-service training in reading and writing once every seven or eight years. With such a design and with the turnover of teachers in a district, an individual might easily work for five or six years in a district and not have any in-service training in reading. Professional development in literacy should occur to some extent every year in all school districts in relation to reading in the content areas as well as to beginning reading as a foundation for learning.

Summer and intersession programs provide excellent teacher training opportunities. Workshops can be coupled with in-classroom coaching experiences that provide guided practice, foster teacher expertise, and accelerate student learning. With this model, teacher coaches can be trained and in turn become lead teachers and peer coaches during the regular school year.

As training is designed, attention needs to be given to areas of beginning reading in which the research base for successful practices is becoming clearer. As described in the first part of this advisory, new research is being completed regularly. Valid findings need to be incorporated into professional development activities to inform teachers and contribute as soon as possible to program development and student learning. Topics that should be emphasized include phonemic awareness; systematic, explicit phonics; beginning writing; spelling; and comprehen-

23

sion and higher-order thinking. Teachers should understand these components of a balanced, comprehensive reading program and learn how these components work together to enhance learning.

Effective professional development includes:

- collaborative planning that involves teachers, administrators, and parents in the process;
- long-term, in-depth, sustained activities;
- a variety of strategies, including coaching or mentoring for teachers and administrators to help them apply what they have learned;
- opportunities to reflect on and analyze individual professional practices through model lessons, collegial support discussions, visits to promising programs, and so forth; and
- discussions of research findings through book clubs and teacher research or study groups.

Teachers, teacher educators, and curriculum specialists are involved in or have access to a variety of statewide opportunities for staff development on early literacy based on the above characteristics. A classroom teacher's most immediate source of help, however, would be from effective local teachers, mentors, specialists, and district leaders in curriculum and instruction.

Program Development

Changes in any program must be carefully and collaboratively planned and supported with appropriate materials as well as training. A two- or three-year design for full program implementation will likely be most successful. Teachers and specialists, like all learners, should not be asked to accommodate tremendous change in a single year, for example. However, if extensive professional development in literacy education is part of every academic year, with time allotted to study, discuss, think, try, revise and coach, then solid, well-grounded changes in teacher strategies and the instructional program can occur quickly, easily, and effectively.

Obviously, a redirection of available funds must also occur to support such program improvement efforts. Besides the targeting of professional development, new and/or redirected funds must also be considered for upgrading the quantity and quality of instructional materials adopted for classroom use and for the school library. The Reading Task Force, for example, recommended a standard of at least 1,500 titles in each classroom.

Conclusion

This program advisory was developed to give structure, organization, and direction to educators and other key individuals to develop a balanced and comprehensive reading program in the schools. It is crucial that the children of California be provided with the most effective instructional methods and materials possible and then be held to high standards of achievement. It is also crucial that the teachers and instructional leaders of California be provided with the most effective professional development programs and appropriate follow-up support and be held accountable for their teaching of reading and writing through a variety of assessment measures. Instruction must be based on appropriate diagnosis that can inform teaching, with a wide repertoire of tools and techniques. Interventions must be at the earliest point possible and be proven in their effectiveness.

As a state, we must not be willing to settle for partial accomplishment of our goals. We must provide a balanced and comprehensive reading and writing program in our schools so that every child will be ensured success as an effective reader, writer and thinker. This is our goal, this is our mandate, and every possible resource must be directed toward this work. For the children of California to succeed in literacy, the teachers of California must be effective. Parents, community, and the entire state must be part of the effort and contribute their support to the teachers and children in our schools. We are in this process together, for the children.

Sample Reading Curriculum Timeline

Preschool Through Eighth Grade

The following suggested timeline is a sample for districts and schools to use in planning for a comprehensive reading program. Each category on the chart represents an essential component of balanced reading instruction, and the examples of activities in each strand represent a range of instruction possible in that component. This timeline is not intended as an exhaustive list but only as a suggested plan for districts to use in developing an effective reading program. Reading and literacy instruction also are integral components of middle school and secondary programs.

Reading programs should be dynamic and powerful and meet the needs of all readers, including encouraging students who are good readers to move ahead and providing intensive support for the lowest achievers. While the components in the timeline are suggestions for teachers regarding classroom activities, it is the students who need to be actively engaged in the learning process. They should have many opportunities to draw on their prior knowledge and respond critically to what they read and write based on their own experiences.

It is important to remember, too, that reading does not occur in isolation. Reading, writing, speaking, and listening are linked as a child becomes competent in English–language arts. There should be a deliberate forging of connections among grades, content areas, and all members of the education community whose work affects children and their reading abilities. The continuum of instruction should be seamless while recognizing and adjusting for individual needs based on each child's actual learning.

From *Every Child a Reader: The Report of the California Reading Task Force*. Sacramento: California Department of Education, 1995.

Sample Reading Curriculum Timeline

1 ORAL LANGUAGE, LISTENING, AND SPEAKING

Strand	Preschool	Kindergarten	First Grade—Fall	First Grade—Spring	Second and Third Grades	Fourth Through Eighth Grades
Listening and Discussion	Listens to a variety of texts, both fiction and nonfiction Discusses a variety of texts, both fiction and nonfiction Listens to directions					
Oral Language	Storytelling Retelling Rhyme and songs	Reads aloud	Explanations Poetry Group discussions Plays Recitations Expressive language Choral reading Reader's theater		Reports Public speaking and debate	

2 AWARENESS OF SOUND, SYMBOL, AND STRUCTURE

Strand	Preschool	Kindergarten	First Grade—Fall	First Grade—Spring	Second and Third Grades	Fourth Through Eighth Grades
Phonemic Awareness	Hears separate words Recognizes rhyming words	Analogies (e.g., "cat to fat") Hears syllables Recognizes word family patterns Matches sounds of words Blends phonemes	More complex analogies		More complex segmenting, blending, and transposition	

NOTE: To avoid repetition in this chart, each activity is first listed during the year it is introduced, and the shaded area that follows represents the subsequent years in which that activity occurs.

AWARENESS OF SOUND, SYMBOL, AND STRUCTURE (Continued)

Strand	Preschool	Kindergarten	First Grade—Fall	First Grade—Spring	Second and Third Grades	Fourth Through Eighth Grades
Phonemic Awareness (Continued)			Hears and segments initial and final phonemes	Hears and segments initial, final, and medial phonemes		
Print Awareness	Reading-like behaviors Recognizes signs and print in the environment Scribbles	Recognizes own name Handles books Has concept of letter/word directionality Writes some letters/words Understands initial concepts about print	Understands more complex concepts about print			
Syntactic Awareness	Uses oral language structure	Understands how words, phrases, sentences work Begins to use book language	Understands and extends book language Reads punctuation Understands sentence and story structure Paragraphing Beginning grammar	More complex grammar	Formal language structure of stories, poems, books, newspapers, etc.	

3 SKILLS INTEGRATION

Strand	Preschool	Kindergarten	First Grade—Fall	First Grade—Spring	Second and Third Grades	Fourth Through Eighth Grades
Letter Recognition	Exposure to letter names and alphabet	Knows most letter names and shapes	Knows all letter names and shapes			

NOTE: To avoid repetition in this chart, each activity is first listed during the year it is introduced, and the shaded area that follows represents the subsequent years in which that activity occurs.

SKILLS INTEGRATION (Continued)

Strand	Preschool	Kindergarten	First Grade–Fall	First Grade–Spring	Second and Third Grades	Fourth Through Eighth Grades
Recognizing High-Frequency Words (Irregular and Regular)		Knows some sight words	Evidences self-correction and self-monitoring Automatically recognizes 50 high-frequency words		Recognizes 150 high-frequency words	Recognizes most high-frequency words
Word Families, Word Patterns, Word Play		Attention to word beginnings and endings (e.g., "C and - at," "M and - at")	Recognizes basic word families and patterns	Recognizes most primary word families and patterns		
Phonics, Decoding, Word Attack		Knows some letter/sound correspondences Recognizes own name Uses syllabication	Basic letter/sound correspondences Knows decoding strategies Sounds out words Compares similar words Breaks words into smaller words Looks for word parts/affixes Uses graphophonemic, semantic, and syntactic cues	Complex letter/sound correspondences Continued development of decoding ability	Remaining letter/sound correspondences	

NOTE: To avoid repetition in this chart, each activity is first listed during the year it is introduced, and the shaded area that follows represents the subsequent years in which that activity occurs.

4 READING AND COMPREHENSION STRATEGIES

Strand	Preschool	Kindergarten	First Grade–Fall	First Grade–Spring	Second and Third Grades	Fourth Through Eighth Grades
Reading to, with, and by Children	Stories and nursery rhymes are read to children	Stories and informational texts are read to children				
		Reads specifically designed books and other appropriate materials		Reads narrative and information texts as the primary learning strategy		
		Individual or small group reading of simple texts				
			Reads 100 to 200 little books		Reads 25 to 35 grade-appropriate books each year from accepted fiction and nonfiction lists	
				Reads and discusses stories, magazines, and informational texts from anthologies and reading series	Has in-depth discussions, uses a variety of genres, and reads in subject-matter areas	
		Shared reading				
		Guided reading				
		Independent reading				
	Reads at home Uses the library					
			Silent, sustained reading			
Comprehension strategies	Uses picture books and simple story books in reading for meaning		Reads for meaning	Organized discussion about commonly read stories		
			Beginning comprehension strategies, predicting, and connecting to what is known		Advanced strategic reading	
			Summarizing and visualizing		Advanced summarizing and visualizing	

NOTE: To avoid repetition in this chart, each activity is first listed during the year it is introduced, and the shaded area that follows represents the subsequent years in which that activity occurs.

READING AND COMPREHENSION STRATEGIES (Continued)

Strand	Preschool	Kindergarten	First Grade–Fall	First Grade–Spring	Second and Third Grades	Fourth Through Eighth Grades
Fluency		Reads familiar materials Oral reading	Uses expression and phrasing			
Recreational Reading		Fiction (e.g., fairy tales, poetry, stories) Different genres (e.g., poetry) Nonfiction (e.g., true stories, nature stories, career stories) Multicultural literature				
Content-Area Reading		Math reading (e.g., counting books) Social studies reading	Reads newspapers and magazines	All content fields (e.g., math, social studies, science)	Reflective/transformative literature and critical responses Uses reference materials	

5 WRITING, VOCABULARY, AND SPELLING

Strand	Preschool	Kindergarten	First Grade–Fall	First Grade–Spring	Second and Third Grades	Fourth Through Eighth Grades
Writing, Encoding	Pretend writing Makes signs Scribbles	Writes words (temporary spelling) Writes own name Group-dictated stories	Uses basic mechanics (e.g., punctuation, capitalization) Uses beginning grammar		Uses standard conventions of writing Uses more complex grammar	

NOTE: To avoid repetition in this chart, each activity is first listed during the year it is introduced, and the shaded area that follows represents the subsequent years in which that activity occurs.

WRITING, VOCABULARY, AND SPELLING (Continued)

Strand	Preschool	Kindergarten	First Grade—Fall	First Grade—Spring	Second and Third Grades	Fourth Through Eighth Grades
Writing, Encoding (Continued)		Letter formation		Writes narratives, expository texts (e.g., organizing information for a report)	Writes more complex narratives, reports, description	
					Composition (e.g., sentence structure and paragraph)	
			Handwriting			
		Composes a variety of stories		Composes a variety of texts		
		Hears and records sounds in words				
Vocabulary	Gains word meaning from oral discussion and explanation					
		Learns some new words from reading and writing			Learns most new words from reading	
		Builds simple words with magnetic letters and other manipulatives	Constructs words from given parts	Constructs more complex word structures	Learns terms from context	
					Learns word roots and affixes	
					Uses synonyms and antonyms	
Spelling	Makes signs	Temporary spelling	Transitions to conventional spelling	Corrects spelling in final drafts	Individualized spelling program based on words in reading and writing	
					Tricky spelling words	
			Spells words in reading lessons		Spelling lists organized by sound theme and common parts	
				Spells sound families and high-frequency words		
				Works on individualized problem words		

NOTE: To avoid repetition in this chart, each activity is first listed during the year it is introduced, and the shaded area that follows represents the subsequent years in which that activity occurs.

Bibliography

Adams, M. J. *Beginning to Read: Thinking and Learning About Print.* Cambridge, MA: MIT Press, 1990.

Adams, M. J., Treiman, R., and Pressley, M. "Reading, Writing, and Literacy." In *Handbook of Child Psychology,* edited by I. Sigel and A. Renninger, Vol. 4: *Child Psychology in Practice.* New York: Wiley, 1996.

Anderson, R., Hiebert, E., Scott, J., and Wilkinson, I. *Becoming a Nation of Readers: The Report of the Commission on Reading.* Washington, D.C: National Institute of Education, U.S. Department of Education, 1984.

Barr, M., and Syverson, M. *California Learning Record: A Handbook for Teachers, K–6.* San Diego, CA: University of California at San Diego Bookstore, 1994.

Bruck, M. "Word Recognition Skills of Adults with Childhood Diagnoses of Dyslexia." *Developmental Psychology,* Vol. 26 (1990), 439–454.

Clay, M. *Becoming Literate: The Construction of Inner Control.* Portsmouth, NH: Heinemann, 1991.

Clay, M. *An Observation Survey of Early Literacy Achievement.* Portsmouth, NH: Heinemann, 1993.

Ehri, L. "Reconceptualizing the Development of Sight Word Reading and Its Relationship to Recoding." In *Reading Acquisition,* edited by P. B. Gough, L. C. Ehri, and R. Treiman, pp. 107–143. Hillsdale, NJ: Erlbaum Associates, 1992.

Every Child a Reader: The Report of the California Reading Task Force. Sacramento: California Department of Education, 1995.

Holdaway, D. *The Foundations of Literacy.* Sydney, Australia: Ashton Scholastic, 1979.

Nagy, W., Herman, P., and Anderson, R. "Learning Words from Context." *Reading Research Quarterly,* Vol. 19 (1985), 304–330.

Perfetti, C. *Reading Ability.* New York: Oxford University Press, 1985.

Rack, J., Snowling, M., and Olson, R. "The Nonword Reading Deficit in Developmental Dyslexia: A Review." *Reading Research Quarterly,* Vol. 27 (1992), 28–53.

Read, C. *Children's Creative Spelling.* London: Routledge and Kegan Paul, 1986.

Rising to the Challenge: A New Agenda for California Schools and Communities. Denver, CO: Education Commission of the States, 1995.

Share, D., and Stanovich, K. "Cognitive Processes in Early Reading Development: Accommodating Individual Differences into a Mode of Acquisition." *Issues in Education: Contributions from Educational Psychology,* Vol. 1 (1995), 1–57.

Shefelbine, J. *Learning and Using Phonics in Beginning Reading.* New York: Scholastic, Inc., 1995.

Stanovich, K. "Matthew Effects in Reading: Some Consequences of Individual Differences in the Acquisition of Literacy." *Reading Research Quarterly,* Vol. 21 (1986), 360–407.

Stanovich, K. "Does Reading Make You Smarter? Literacy and the Development of Verbal Intelligence." In *Advances in Child Development and Behavior,* edited by H. Reese, Vol. 24, pp. 133–180. San Diego, CA: Academic Press, 1993.

Stanovich, K. "Toward an Interactive Compensatory Model of Individual Differences in the Development of Reading Fluency." *Reading Research Quarterly,* Vol. 16 (1980), 32–71.

Treiman, R. *Beginning to Spell: A Study of First-Grade Children.* New York: Oxford University Press, 1993.

Vellutino, F. "Introduction to Three Studies on Reading Acquisition: Convergent Findings on Theoretical Foundations of Code-oriented Versus Whole Language Approaches to Reading Instruction." *Journal of Educational Psychology,* Vol. 83 (1991), 437–443.

Yopp, H. "Developing Phonemic Awareness in Young Children." *The Reading Teacher,* Vol. 45 (1992), 696–703.

R96-21 (Fifth printing) 02-0758 10-96 10 M